"Sometimes God Has a Kid's Face"

Sr. Mary Rose McGeady

Covenant House

DEDICATED
to the over one million children
we have had the privilege of serving
these past 38 years - kids who were
scared, cold, hungry, alone and, most of all,
desperate to find someone who cared.
We are honored to have helped.

Table of Contents

Introduction   5

"Playtime is over, kid," he said.   9

"Is it OK if I stay an extra night?" she asked.   17

"I was getting beaten up all the time," he said.   23

"I figured you were going to kick me out, too."   29

"I used to be from somewhere, but I'm not from anywhere anymore."   33

"My dad says it's 'cause I'm stupid."   41

"If you tell anyone ... we'll kill you."   47

"His favorite trick was to beat me with a broom handle."   53

"He seemed to have this thing about my brother," she said.   59

"I want to be a somebody, some day," she said.   63

"I was afraid he'd kill me."   69

"As he walked off into the darkness, we wondered if we would ever see him again.   75

"It's hopeless ... I'm hopeless."   81

"I finally decided that I couldn't take it anymore."   87

"Faith Into Action"   93

EPILOGUE   96

Where Do We Go From Here?   99

Family Survival Guide   100

Introduction

"Can I stay here?" the tiny girl standing on our doorstep asked me last night.

"I hear you let kids sleep here, if they don't have any place else to go," she said. "Well … I don't," she said. *"I don't have anything," she said.*

She stood there, and looked at me, and I could feel my heart beginning to break into a million little pieces. She was seventeen, dressed in dirty jeans and a t-shirt that hadn't seen a washer and dryer in a couple of weeks.

But if you had been with me at the doorstep last night, the thing you would have noticed most of all were her eyes. "Please, please, please don't turn your back on me," her eyes begged. "Everyone turns their back on me, everyone ignores me," they said. "I've never been loved …never been cared for my whole life. Please … will you at least pretend you care," her eyes said.

Her eyes were too sad and too hollow and too empty to cry. But they said more in those five seconds than most kids will ever say in a lifetime.

*Years ago I didn't know that there were girls like this on our streets … **literally a million innocent, homeless American kids** … lost and alone and sometimes dying on America's streets.*

But then I learned the cold truth, from an extraordinary woman of God named Sister Mary Rose McGeady. My life, and theirs, have never been the same.

I'm not sure if you've ever heard the name Sister Mary Rose McGeady, but to tens of thousands of American kids, she is their Guardian Angel, their Mother Teresa.

For thirteen years, while much of America was either unaware or unconcerned that homeless children were dying on our streets, Sr. Mary Rose stood watch on the doorstep of a place called Covenant House – a crisis shelter for homeless and runaway kids. And every night, as she opened her arms wider, more and more kids found her, and came to her. In droves.

At the beginning of her service as President of Covenant House, Sister Mary Rose and her staff were welcoming about a thousand homeless kids every night – providing food, clothing, medicine and a warm bed to every lost child who knocked on the doors. By the time she retired, the stream of kids being rescued in Covenant House shelters across America had more than doubled.

"Sometimes God Has Kid's Face" is Sister Mary Rose's incredible story of her life with these kids. Told through her eyes. In her words. Straight from the alleyways and dead end streets they lived, and sometimes, died on. Through life-changing moment after life-changing moment.

As the current President of Covenant House, and the custodian of her legacy, I am honored to share this story on her behalf, and mostly, on behalf of the children she so lovingly served. Sister Mary Rose lived and died every day with the successes and failures of our kids… and she saw God in the dirty, exhausted faces of the kids finding the open doors of Covenant House.

I still think of her whenever I stand on the doorstep of Covenant House, peering into the eyes of a homeless child. And I still smile whenever I think of her opening her arms, and leading kids inside.

Kevin Ryan

President, Covenant House

I do not consider myself to be a follower,
just a lonely deserted soul in a barbaric city,
who walks his own treacherous path in life.

Written by Brian,
after six months alone
on the street

Chapter 1

"Playtime is over, kid," he said.

The dark car hurtled down the street, across the avenue from our Outreach van. Suddenly, the back door opened and a body flew out of the car and rolled several times on the asphalt.

The car screeched to a halt, but the tall, thin girl who had tumbled out got up and ran towards our van. "Help me! Help me!" she cried, with blood running down her face and arms. The car raced towards our van, stopped for a long pause, and then finally sped away.

"Are they following us?" she asked, her body glued to the floor of our van.

"Please tell me they're gone," she cried.

"They'll kill me if they ever catch me," she said.

She looked up from the floor of our van, tears running down her cheeks. And blood everywhere.

Even though it was pitch black, her eyes still pierced the darkness, and grabbed onto each of us. They were the kind of eyes you don't often see, and never forget; eyes that darted and danced and literally begged — pleaded — for safety.

"You're safe now," we said. "You really are."

"I hope you're right," her eyes seemed to scream back. "I've heard that before. I hope you're right ..."

The first few hours back at the shelter were like a scene out of an emergency room. She was a mess; her clothes tattered and torn, her body bruised and bleeding. For a few minutes, we feared she may have broken her left arm when she landed and rolled on the street outside, but our doctors determined it was only (only?) a severe bruise.

As bad as Sandra looked on the outside though, it was her insides that hurt the most. All the while, we cared for her, and soothed her, and bandaged her, tears and moans of agony cried out to all of us. She was at times almost inconsolable — a young kid, barely seventeen, rocking and screaming on a couch, unable to stop the pain inside.

Once we heard her story, we were able to understand why ...

"Do you think I'm safe here Sister?" she asked me later that night. "I mean, really safe?"

"You are," I said. "No one can get to you here. You have my word on that."

"Who are you running from?" I asked.

"It's a guy," she said. "I thought he ... I thought he loved me," she said. "But I guess he really didn't." Tears began to form in her eyes again.

"I met him last year. I've been on the street for a long time," she said. "I didn't want to be on the street ... you know, it's pretty tough out there ... but I was. And then I met Nate ... he said he'd help me," she said.

"I wanted to believe in him," she said. *"I mean, I've always wanted to find someone I could believe in.*

"You got to understand, Sister, it's been pretty rough for me, for a long time," she said. The words began to pour out, fast and furious. There was so much pain in her soul, so much torment she needed to unload before she could ever even hope of healing ...

"My father died right after I was born, and then my mother moved in with another guy. He ... he did things to me that I don't really want to talk about," she said. (I could see the words sexual abuse written all over her tormented face.) "I was only six years old when he did that stuff to me," she said. "Only six....

"After that, I was taken to another home, and then another, and another. I bumped around a lot of places, until I decided maybe I'd be better off on the street. That wasn't any good, either," she said. "And then I met Nate, and he said he'd help me.

"I wasn't sure what to do, but he seemed so nice and I didn't have any other place to go, so I moved in. Pretty stupid, huh," she said, looking at me.

I guess to some people what she did might have sounded kind of dumb, but I had seen her face and heard her story a thousand times before, and I knew better. I mean, she was 17 and all alone on the street, and hungry and cold and wondering how she was going to live and if she even deserved to live ... and someone offered to take her inside, and rescue her.

What would you or I do if we were in that impossible situation? What would anyone do?

"No, I understand why you did that," I said. A look of relief spread across her face. "Thanks," she mumbled softly. "I needed to hear that," she said.

"For the first few weeks, it was nice living with

him. He was very nice to me, and he fed me, and he said he really loved me. I thought maybe I had finally found something special," she said.

"But then one night, he came back to the apartment, and he was really mad," she said. "He told me that I was costing him a lot of money, and eating too much of his food. Then he said I was stealing from him.

"At first I thought he was kidding. But when I looked in his eyes, I saw something there that really scared me.

"I wasn't stealing, Sister ... I mean, you got to believe me ... but I couldn't change his mind. He kept telling me he was going to throw me out.

"Then he came up with a new plan."

Sandra turned away from me. Her shoulders slumped. When she turned back, tears were welling in her eyes.

"He wanted me to be a prostitute. He said I could earn lots of money. I wanted to say no, but he was scaring me. And I knew that I didn't have any money. I couldn't bear the thought of going out on the street, and I told him so.

"That's when things started to get really bad," she said.

"He came up to me, and pulled out a knife, and held it to my throat. 'Playtime is over, kid' he said. 'Either you get out there and start earning your way, or I'm going to kill you' he said.

"He wasn't kidding, Sister," she said. (I knew he

wasn't. I'd seen it a hundred times before.)

"So I did what he wanted."

Sandra shrank before my eyes. I don't know how she got her lanky frame into so small a ball on the chair, but she did. It was several minutes before she spoke again.

"I did some awful things, Sister. When I think back, I can't believe the things I did. I cry every time I remember. I wish I could go back, you know?

"I wish I could go back and take away those things so I don't have to think of myself this way. I wish I could be the way I was. Will I ever be able to do that, Sister?"

After more than ten years at Covenant House, that question still brings tears to my eyes. "Will I ever be able to go back to the way I was before?"

It must be the saddest thing a child can say.

I mean, we all end up with regrets in this life. None of us escape that. But for someone like Sandra to have so big a regret so early in life is heartbreaking.

And there is so little that any of us here on earth can do to help.

"Sandra, I know you wish you could go back. And you know you can't go back. But it'll be okay. I promise you that.

"You can't go back, but you can go forward. And if you ask God for help, He'll give it to you. I know He will. He'll help you turn what happened to you into a source of strength.

"It won't ever be a pretty memory, but someday

you'll realize how much courage it took for you to escape and come to us. Someday you'll realize that you cared enough about yourself to stop living that way. Someday you'll be proud of yourself for that.

"And though you are ashamed of yourself now, I promise you that God still sees you as His little girl. He never stops seeing us that way. No matter what happens to us."

Sandra looked up at me. Her face was drenched in tears. "No matter what?" she said in a ten-year-old's voice.

"No matter what," I said.

We talked a little longer, and then Sandra went up to her room. I said a prayer that she would sleep well and wake up feeling like God's little girl. I say that kind of prayer often for my kids. They are so young, and so much has happened to them that makes them feel so ashamed.

I mean, on the street, these kids are forced to make choices that you and I can't imagine. And so often, they are choosing between one thing they'll regret forever and another thing they'll regret forever. By the time they come to Covenant House, they carry a load of regret so heavy it physically bows them.

But I truly believe what I told Sandra. God can lift that heavy burden from them. I've seen it happen again and again. So that's why I pray for them. I hope you will, too.

Run Away

Scared and cold,
first night on the streets
Your body hurts
from your head to your feet

You miss school,
not the work — it's the friends
Thinking what you'll say
when they ask
where you've been

Gota dollar-fifty,
every penny gotta spend
Make a wrong move ... Boom —
your life comes to an end.

> *Daniel, 16*
> *a kid on the street*

Chapter 2

"Is it OK if I stay an extra night?" she ask...

"I'm not afraid because I *don't* know what's out there, Sister.

"I'm scared for a different reason," she said.

"I'm scared because I *do* know what's out there. I know … and I'm scared. That's why I can't leave. I just can't."

Kathleen stood in the doorway of her room at Covenant House, with her hands planted squarely on either side of the doorframe as if she were afraid I was going to try to physically drag her from the room.

Her bright blue eyes were wide with fear and determination.

"Kathleen, it's OK. Someone will go with you. You won't be alone. You said you wanted to do this."

"I know. I know I did. And I do. I know I need to be on my own. I mean, I know I can't live here forever. But can't I stay a little longer?

"You know, I always thought things were bad at home. When my dad would get drunk and beat me and things like that. Or when my mom would be drugged out and scary.

"But it was even worse on the street. I mean, everyone was drunk or drugged out. And they all wanted something ... know what I mean?

"I don't know if I can describe it, but I don't think

I was ever, even for a second, NOT scared when I was on the street."

She paused to look deep into my eyes. She wanted to make sure I was following her. That I understood. That I knew — absolutely knew — the incredible fear she felt inside.

I looked into her eyes and tried my best to comfort her. I could feel my mind racing a mile a minute, imagining what was causing the terror bubbling inside her.

It wasn't too hard imagining what those once innocent eyes had seen on the streets.

I've seen those eyes a thousand times before….

Like so many of our kids, she had run to the streets to escape a wretched and dangerous life at home. At first, I'm sure Kathleen's eyes could only see better days ahead — a life finally freed from the day-to-day abuse and terror that was slowly killing her at home.

But then reality of the street caught up with her.

It always does. Always.

After only a couple of days, she began to realize that she was now utterly and completely alone. What had once been the world's simplest questions became impossible to answer …

"Where am I going to sleep tonight?"

"What am I going to eat?"

"Can I make it on my own?"

"Is there anyone in this world who cares?"

Her world — her entire huge world — was now suddenly empty of even one person she could lean on.

Can you imagine what that must be like? Can you imagine how that might change the way you would see the world?

Her eyes began to see trash cans filled with old food — and now she began to wonder if she should just take a bite. Her stomach ached, she was so hungry. Maybe just a bite.

Her eyes saw old men asking for unspeakable favors — and she suddenly began to wonder if maybe, just maybe, she could close her eyes for a moment and give herself up. Her pockets were empty, she desperately needed money, she had to do something.

Her eyes suddenly began to see a world no decent person — let alone a kid — should ever have to see and face. A world that was dark, and dangerous, and unforgiving, and unfriendly and unrelenting. A world that literally chews up and devours innocent kids.

That's what I'm sure Kathleen's eyes had seen on the street.

And it's precisely why they were laced with fear now. The very idea of leaving Covenant House — and maybe one day seeing any part of that awful world again — froze her with terror.

It happens to all our kids. Some of them, the strongest ones, can somehow forget about it, or at least put it back into an airtight part of their memory, where they never have to revisit it again.

For a lot of the others, kids like Kathleen, it's harder to forget. One of the biggest lessons we all learn at Covenant House about saving kids is that we first have to somehow save them from their fears.

That's what Kathleen needed most of all.

"I know why you feel this way, Kathleen," I said.

"I know how tough it can be going back out there.

"We can take it a little slower, if you'd like."

Her eyes softened for a moment, and seemed to relax.

"But I want you to realize something very important," I said. "It's different now. You're different now. You're entire support system is different now," I said.

"When you go outside these doors again, it will not be the same world, and it will not be the same you. You'll always know that we're here for you," I told her. "You didn't know that before."

She nodded her head quietly to say she understood. Pools of tears were beginning to form in her eyes.

"And you have someone else you can rely on more than ever, and that's you," I said. "You know now how good you are, and how smart you are, and how much you have to offer this world," I said. "You know how much we all believe in you."

"You're right," she whispered very softly. "I didn't really know that before."

She wiped away the tears that were now streaming down her face. I could see she now understood that her time at Covenant House had truly changed everything in her world. And inside her, too.

"Is it still OK if I stay an extra night?" she asked. "Just one more," she said. "Then I'll be all right."

"I'd like that," I said.

"Thanks," she said.

She turned for a second to leave, but then turned back and gave me a quick, self-conscious hug. "Bye," she said.

Tomorrow, her new life begins.

I'll be praying for her extra hard.

Just as surely as she couldn't be beginning a new life without Covenant House, she wouldn't be starting a new life without your help, too. Please … will you pray for her if you can?

Kathleen hasn't been outside of Covenant House since she came to us. I'm worried about her, but I think she's going to do OK. She has a long way to go and she is really terrified of being alone again, but I think she will make it.

Thank you for praying for her too, and for doing all you've done to help her so far.

My precious Jesus,

*I am hurting. To write everything
would fill this book. You know my
troubles, you know my questions
and you know my answers. Please
help me. Give me strength and
please give me what I need to be
happy. Please love and take care
of my cats and all the hungry
people and creatures of the world.*

> *A prayer written
> by a kid in our
> Chapel*

Chapter 3

"I was getting beaten up all the time," he said.

The boy placed both his hands gently over his eyes, and then plopped his body onto the couch in the middle of our crisis shelter floor.

For the first few minutes, he was a bundle of nerves and reckless anxiety. He burrowed his eyes deeper into his hands. He rocked back and forth, in fits and starts. He sighed, and grunted syllables I couldn't quite discern.

But slowly, as the seconds ticked off, I began to see his mind and his heart drift away from us. The hands that just moments ago were pushing against his eyes, now stopped. The nervous rocking eased, until his body was now swaying back and forth in a slow, rhythmic motion.

And then, as the frown that had been on his face finally gave way to a contented smile, he moved his right hand away from his eyes …

… and placed his thumb inside his mouth.

It was the most relaxed I had ever seen him.

It was a long time before Joey woke up, and returned back to our world. From the quizzical look on his face, I could tell he was surprised to see me still standing there.

"I'm sorry I did that, just then," he said. "You know, hid from you like that."

"I didn't mean to be rude or anything, he said. "I guess it's just something that helps me deal with stuff," he said.

"You know, sometimes, when I feel really uncomfortable, I just have to close my eyes and go away. Usually it's only for a couple of minutes, but sometimes I lose track of time."

Joey leaned forward on his chair. Then he stood up. Then he walked around to the back of the chair. Then he came back around to the front. Now that his eyes were open to see the world, he had trouble staying still to deal with it …

"I understand," I said. "Don't think anything of it," I said. "Do you want to tell me how you ended up here?" I asked.

"No special reason," he said, the nervous look in his eyes betraying his words. "I … I guess I just couldn't take it anymore."

"What happened?" I asked.

He got up again, walked around the couch, and plopped himself back down. "Well, I … I had this uncle, who … well, he used to do stuff to me. You know, sexual stuff," he said.

"He used to come over when my parents weren't around, and he would do all this stuff to me," he said.

"Did you tell your parents?"

"Yuh, I told them, but they didn't believe me, you know," he said. "It wasn't like they cared anyway," he said.

"My parents used to argue all the time. And they

always seemed mad at me," he said.

"When they got real mad it used to be pretty bad. They used to beat me, and stuff," he said. "I could show you the marks if you'd like."

I nodded and let him know that wouldn't be necessary.

"So ... I guess this is going to sound real stupid to you ... I used to try to get away, you know," he said. "I'd go up to my room, and just go inside the closet. I used to go in there for hours," he said. "It was the only place where I felt safe."

"Then, about a year ago, it just got to be too much. I was getting beaten up all the time," he said. "And all that other stuff, too," he said.

"I couldn't stand it anymore," he said. "I just had to leave.

"I thought it would be better, but ..." his voice began to choke up and it trailed off and was lost. He didn't have to finish the sentence — I'd heard kids tell me this a thousand times before.

Out of his house, away from his closet, Joey found a world most of us will never see — a street life filled with dead ends, and abuse, and terror and relentless pain.

He bent his head down and hid his hands in his face. I think his body and heart wanted to cry, but there weren't any tears left. I put my hand on his shoulder, and told him what a great kid he really was....

He's ours now. His family has abused him, and the streets have nearly destroyed him. Like so many of the kids we'll see this coming year (and we estimate we'll see more than 60,000 kids at our doorstep!!!), Joey's insides have almost been destroyed.

It's not the physical pain he feels that most worries me (although the hunger and sickness he carries are almost enough to destroy any kid).

It's Joey's 'insides' that break my heart — the fact he has been emotionally destroyed.

To kids like Joey, the real world is so harsh — so unforgiving, so devoid of hope and love and compassion — that they must create another fantasy world just to survive.

Given where he's been, and what he's seen, and how he's hurt, it makes perfect sense for Joey to separate himself from the real world — because his fantasy world is the only place he has ever known peace and contentment.

Of course, this makes our world at Covenant House increasingly difficult. During my ten years here, the number of kids like Joey has literally mushroomed. These kids come to us with a whole range of special needs, needs that require more help in more ways than the usual homeless kid. (The 'usual homeless kid' … I wince just writing those words.)

More than any other kids, children like Joey come to us literally dangling by a thread, totally unattached to anyone or anything he can call his own.

Either we save him, or the world will forever lose him. His situation is that precarious — our responsibility to him is that serious.

I know you and Joey have never met, and you probably never will. But you, and God, are the very best things in his life right now. Your prayers, and your helping hands, and your support of this lifesaving mission, are literally the only things pulling Joey back from the precipice right now.

Our Love

Sometimes I wonder how people
    judge our love,
They never seem to notice that it
    comes from Heaven above.
But if our love is strong and true
    and solid to the soul,
Then listening to them is not
    what we'll do.
Our love will be bold.
The love we have will shine
    through storms,
No matter how rough the times.
Forever and ever, we'll be
    together like the sun.
Yes, it will shine.

Written by a
Covenant House kid

Chapter 4

"I figured you were going to kick me out, too."

"Are you going to kick me out, too, Sister?" the homeless kid said.

"I mean, I guess I don't blame you if you want to," he said.

"I'm used to being kicked out."

"Of course not, Michael," I said. "Why would we kick you out?"

"Well, I know my roommate complained about me snoring. He kept waking me up all night to tell me to stop snoring. And the roommate I had before that complained, too.

"I just figured it was probably going to happen again and I was going to get kicked out."

"What do you mean, 'again'?" I asked.

"Well, you know … that's why I got kicked out of my own house. My mother and my brothers all said I snored too much. They said they couldn't take it. So they kicked me out.

"I guess I don't blame them," he said. "I guess it must be pretty bad. And my brothers and I all slept in one room, and they said they couldn't sleep with me snoring all the time.

"That's why I figured it was going to happen again now," he said. "I figured you were going to kick me out, too."

"No, Michael, we are NOT going to kick you out for snoring. We're going to figure out how to help you deal with this, but we are NOT going to kick you out. I promise you that."

Michael sighed. His cheeks turned slightly red.

"I guess it's because I'm so fat, huh? That's probably why I snore so bad. That's what my mother said. She said I snored so bad because I was so fat and lazy.

"I guess it's true. I just don't know what to do about it."

Michael looked at me, hoping I had the answers. I didn't, of course. Except that I knew that this kid pretty desperately needed someone to care about him. He needed someone to see beyond this one problem and find the child of God underneath.

The idea that a kid would be kicked out of his house for snoring might seem almost comical.

But there is nothing funny about Michael's life.

The truth is, Michael is badly overweight and he does snore very loudly. More than one roommate of his at Covenant House has asked to be reassigned to another room.

But can this be a reason to throw away a person? In all His endless mercy, could even God forgive us for that?

When Michael came to us, he was about the most dejected kid I've ever seen. What do you think when your mother kicks you out of your home, your family, because you snore too loudly?

Now here's the most heartbreaking part of this

story. After I talked with Michael, I told him we would take him to a doctor and see if anything could be done about his snoring. But in the meantime, we gave him a room by himself.

The next morning, and in the days after that, he was a changed person. He said he felt better than he ever had before. He had energy. He was optimistic. He was cheerful.

It turns out that Michael had not had a good night's sleep in years. Between his siblings waking him up, and even his roommates at Covenant House, the poor kid had never slept more than an hour or so at a time.

Within a week after we gave him his own room, he had found a good job. He was even talking about going to college.

I wanted to tell you his story because I think it shows the bizarre ways that our society can hurt kids. And it also shows how easy it is sometimes to turn their lives around if someone just stops to understand them and figure out what their problems are. If someone just stops for a minute to actually love them.

Dear God,

*I just want someone to love me, someone
to talk to when I need to talk. Someone to
cry on when I need to cry. Most of all
someone to love me and walk as far
as they wish through my life. Amen.*

> *A prayer written
> by a kid in our
> Covenant House chapel*

Chapter 5

*"I used to be from somewhere, but
I'm not from anywhere anymore."*

"I heard that you could help me," she said.

"Maybe you could just let me have a sandwich, and I'll get out of your hair," she said.

"I really don't want to get in your way."

I looked into her sad, no-one-loves-me eyes, and felt a stake piercing my heart. She was a little kid, maybe 14 or 15 or 16 dressed in blue jeans and a sweatshirt that should have been thrown into a trash heap months ago. She was one of those street urchins we see so often, the kind of vagabond/bump-around/hard-knocks kid who mysteriously appears at our doorstep all of a sudden, covered with filth and oozing neglect.

I actually had a hard time guessing her age, there was so much dirt and pain smeared across her face.

But there was no mistaking her sweetness and her goodness. Even in the twilight of an early spring evening, we could see those qualities from a mile away. You would have loved her the second you laid eyes on her....

"Maybe I could even get a little something to drink too," she said. "If it wouldn't be a problem?"

"Please, come in," I said. "We've got plenty of food. Please, we're glad you are here," I said.

She tried to smile back, but I could tell she wasn't too used to smiling. She nodded a small nod, and quickly walked in.

"There's a cafeteria down the hall," I said. "Why don't we just take a minute to wash our hands and get cleaned up, and I'll take you there myself," I said. "My name is Sister Mary Rose — what's yours?" I said.

"Dana," she said.

"Where are you from?" I asked.

"Nowhere," she said.

"What do you mean?" I said.

"Well ... I mean I used to be from somewhere, but I'm not from anywhere anymore," she said. "Is this the way to the cafeteria?" she said.

I took her by the hand, and led her to a sink and a bar of soap, where she could clean off the layers of dirt camped out on her hands and arms. It wasn't a simple cleaning — it was a good forty-five seconds before I could see her red, chafed skin underneath. Once her hands dried, I hurried her to the cafeteria, where hot soup and sandwiches were lined neatly on the countertops.

Dana grabbed three of each, rushed politely over to the first empty table, and dove in. It took her all of five minutes to clean off the entire tray.

"Thanks a lot," she said. "That was really good," she said. "Maybe I can come back again," she said, half-asking, half-telling, totally hoping I'd say yes.

"You're welcome to stay now," I said. "We've got plenty of clean beds (plenty was a tiny exaggeration, because we're crammed with kids right now, but I was trying as hard as I could to convince her to stay), and you're welcome."

She fidgeted with the napkin, not quite knowing what to say. I could tell she was beginning to get interested...

"Tell me a little about yourself," I said. "How old are you?"

"Sixteen," she said.

"Is there someone we can call to let them know you're here?" I said.

"There used to be," she said. "But not anymore."

"What do you mean?" I asked. "I'd like to help you," I said.

For the longest time, Dana looked at me, twisting her napkin, trying to decide a hundred things all at once. Should I talk? Or should I go? Can I trust this lady? What is this place? Why am I here? How did this happen? Is this someone I can believe in? Where am I going to sleep tonight if I don't sleep here? What should I do? A hundred questions ... all of them way too serious and heartbreaking and urgent for a 16-year-old kid to have to worry about.

Finally, the tears began to form in her eyes, and she decided to take a chance. Dana decided to trust in us.

"I used to live in a real house," she said. "I had a

mother and a father and five brothers," she said. "That was a long time ago," she said.

"Then, last year, my dad decided to leave. He just walked out one day ... he didn't even tell me he was going anywhere ... he just left.

"My mother ... my mother couldn't take it anymore. She tried to get a job ... but it all got to be too much.

"About two months ago, she sat me down and told me I had to leave. 'You're 16, Dana,' she said. 'You're the oldest ... I can't afford all of you ... you're going to have to leave.'

"I looked at her like she was kidding. I mean, leave for what, Sister? Go where? I'm 16 ... it's not like I know a million places to go.

"But my mother kept telling me I had to get out," Dana said. "'You can make it, Dana,' my mother said. 'You're strong like me. Pack up your things. I'm sorry, you have to go.'"

As she poured out her story, the tears began rolling down Dana's cheeks in streams. They were angry, pained, disbelieving tears of a 16-year-old girl who suddenly found herself all alone, on the street, by herself. I grabbed her hand and told her again how glad I was she had found us. She cried some more, and tried to keep on talking ...

"At first ... at first I thought I could make it. I met a boy on the street the first day. I thought maybe I could live with him.

"But ... but that didn't work out ... it ... it didn't work out."

"Where have you been living?" I asked.

"Around," she said. "You know, places," she said, street kid shorthand for alleys, subways, park benches and any other place where a kid can find a spot to sleep.

"We'd love to have you stay with us," I said. "We've got plenty of room," I said.

"I think I'd like that," she said. And then she began to sob uncontrollably. It was a long time before she could stop.

I made sure our staff took extra special care of Dana tonight. We got her some brand-new pajamas, and I made sure she got a room right near one of her counselors, so she could see someone by her all night.

I'm not sure how, or if, she'll be able to sleep tonight.

I mean, I know she's exhausted. She probably hasn't had a restful moment since she was kicked out of her home. But the questions pouring through her head, bouncing back and forth ... I'm sure they're keeping her up tonight.

"How did I ever end up here?" her mind must be asking her. "What did I do wrong? Am I going to always be alone? Am I ever going to be OK? Can I trust these people here? Can I ever trust anyone? Why doesn't my mom love me? Why doesn't anyone love me? Will anyone ever love me?"

I do know one thing. We're going to do everything humanly possible to help her, and try to rebuild her life (and as we're doing all we humanly can, I'm going to be praying extra hard to God for His help too).

I mean, with all the awful, tough, gut-wrenching questions Dana has facing her tonight, the one question she will never have to ask is — "Can I find hope here?"

Dear Heavenly Father,

*Please give me the strength to go on
through my stay at Covenant House.
Give me the wisdom and the knowledge
to do what is right and not wrong.
And please give me the strength to
make the right decisions about the
things that occur. I know I haven't
been making the right decisions,
but I'd like to better that. Life has not
been easy for me through these times,
but I know that you will give me
the strength to go on for I do believe
in you and all you say and do. Amen.*

> *A prayer written
> by a kid in our
> Covenant House chapel*

Chapter 6

"My dad says it's 'cause I'm stupid."

"Where do you live?" I asked him. He said nothing.

"How did you get here?" Silence.

"Where are your parents?" Nothing.

I looked at the young man sitting in front of me, tense, sullen, his body language shouting fear, anger, frustration and hurt ... and yet he remained utterly silent.

His hair was dirty. His clothes even dirtier. We found him living in a park, sleeping on the ground. He was so hungry that when we took him to our cafeteria, he ate enough for five people.

In my office, Zack kept rubbing his arms and his hands as if he couldn't get warm. Maybe the cold was still deep into his bones.

No matter how much I told him that he was welcome here, he still looked scared, doubtful. As if he were wondering when the dream would end and he'd be back in the park, alone and cold.

I asked him a dozen questions. He was silent.

For some reason, I thought of Jesus.

They asked Him to identify himself when they arrested Him.

Jesus refused to answer. They questioned Him further. They asked Him why He was there and where He had come from.

Jesus said little.

I tried to imagine why Jesus was so silent when so much was at stake. Why didn't He make a sermon or tell them a parable? Why didn't He explain His life to them? Why didn't He convince them of His innocence? I have no doubt He could have.

Still, Jesus said nothing.

All his friends had deserted Him. He was accused of crimes He didn't commit. He had no reason to trust the people who interrogated Him. He had no reason to trust anyone.

Even His Father in heaven had rejected His pleas for help.

Jesus must have been scared, angry, frustrated and deeply hurt. Zack wasn't the first person to be struck dumb by heartbreak.

He wasn't the first person who felt he didn't have a friend in the world, and who didn't trust those who said they were trying to help him.

"We're really glad you're here," I told Zack. "I hope you and I can talk at some point, but it doesn't have to be now. I just want you to know you are safe here."

I started to stand up, but Zack shifted his weight and shook his head slowly. Something told me he wanted to talk. I sat back down. I waited. A long time.

"I don't talk so good," he said. "I guess I'm not too smart," he said. "My teacher said I got a problem learning," he said, struggling mightily to say the words. "My dad says I'm just stupid."

It was only a couple of sentences, but I suspected

Zack was telling me an enormous amount about himself.

I asked him more.

He told me his mother died of cirrhosis. He said, "I loved my Mom. I mean, she used to hit me, but only when she was drunk. I wish she didn't die. I really wish she was here."

He said his father and stepmother didn't want him. His grandmother doesn't want him. He has no friends. He flunked out of high school.

"My dad said it was 'cause I'm stupid."

When his mother died and no one would take him in, he lived in the park. He stole food to eat. He didn't eat much.

I'm convinced that every year, God sends me one extra special kid to remind me what Lent is all about.

I mean, Lent is all about self-examination, and things we must ask ourselves, and reckoning, and looking in the mirror to see if we like what's staring back at us.

I'm not the world's biggest fan of Lent, believe me. In fact, I really don't like it. It's not something we're supposed to like, I guess.

It's a time to reflect on how we use the goods of the world, and how we deal with our relationships. It's a time to think back if we're really trying to live a life of love, a time to look under the hood of our souls to make sure everything's running all right and see where the defects are.

Lent is also about resolutions to turn our lives

around, and then begin the painful process of dealing with those resolutions ...

Easy?

It's not, and it's not supposed to be. It's not easy spending forty days staring into the mirror, scrutinizing, writing checklists, grading performance. It's never easy asking ourselves if we're really being as good as we want to be, as virtuous, as steadfast, as understanding. But it's a good time for us, I think. Lent is the one time when we are most in touch with God.

Zack? And kids like Zack?

If Lent is the time when we are most close to God, then kids like Zack must have God's ear pretty well.

I think they know all about Lent, and what God intended for Lent, better than most of us ever will. Zack lives in a perpetual Lent ... a nonstop life of painful reckoning, questioning, excruciating self-examination, of losses.

"What is wrong with me?" our kids find themselves asking, and asking, and asking. "Why am I living like this ... why doesn't anyone love me ... am I suffering because I don't deserve anything better?"

Sometimes, the parallels between what kids like Zack go through and what Jesus went through are startling.

Fear, abandonment, betrayal. Silence.

Lent is painful. But the one great consolation we can draw from all this, is that God gave us Lent to prepare us for Easter. And no one can love the resurrection of Easter — the redemption of Easter — as much as someone who has suffered through Lent.

Maybe that's why I'm so thankful to God during Lent that He has placed our kids here. In Covenant House. Where resurrections are a part of our daily life.

When you and I go through Lent, we know that Easter waits at the other end. It's only 40 days.

Zack, however, has no idea how the story will turn out in the end. He doesn't yet believe that there will be an Easter for him.

I believe there is an Easter coming for Zack. But I wonder if you will help me pray for him. Pray for all the kids of Covenant House who are making their way through their own personal Lent right now. It would be wonderful if you could add this to your own daily prayers.

What a blessing that would be for the kids.

Until the day that our prayers are answered and Zack's Easter comes, we will be here with him.

Learn to Listen

Learn to listen like a teddy bear,
With ears open and mouth closed tight.
Learn to forgive like a teddy bear,
With an open heart, not caring who is right.
Learn to love like a teddy bear,
With arms open and imperfect eyesight.
Do not ask for your life's load lightened,
But for courage to endure.
Do not ask for fulfillment in all your life,
Do not ask for perfection in all you do,
But for the wisdom not to repeat mistakes.
And finally, do not ask for more,
Before saying, "Thank you,"
For what you have already received.
If you're looking for somebody to blame —
Look in the mirror.
There is no challenge that cannot be met,
And dream that cannot be achieved.

Written by one of our
Covenant House kids

Chapter 7

"If you tell anyone ... we'll kill you."

They lurked in the shadows just outside the doors of our shelter — waiting.

Waiting for the moment when they would lure their prey with promises of friendship and safety. It didn't take long.

Two members of the Bloods, a vicious street gang, were on the prowl for a new victim, an innocent girl they could befriend and betray. And she was just around the corner.

She had run away from her abusive home, with nowhere else to go. Now, alone and terrified, friendless and penniless, she was an easy target.

A hand shot out from the shadows and grabbed her gently, at first, by the wrist.

"Hey you, you need a place to stay?"

"Yeah, sure," she answered. After so many cold and lonely nights on the streets of New York, the answer came all too easily.

"Stay with us, we'll take care of you, real good care of you."

Desperate for acceptance, any kind of acceptance, worn down by hunger and lack of sleep, the young runaway was all too eager to accept this innocent offer of friendship.

Now they were joined by a third gang member. A

girl who knew that troubled kids at Covenant House were easy targets.

The trap was set. The prey was inside. And it was about to spring shut ...

The four set off for a cheap hotel, three gang members and the runaway. She wondered "Have I found some friends, at last?"

The answer came all too quickly.

What began with a promise of friendship became a four-day ordeal of streetwalking, beatings and forced imprisonment.

When the young runaway failed to earn money as a teen prostitute for her new-found "friends", they tied her to a chair and took turns beating her with a belt.

"If you tell anyone, if you go to the police, we'll cut you up and we'll kill you."

Finally, she escaped her captors. In spite of their very real threats, she had the courage to go to the police and tell her horrible story.

Thankfully, one member of the Bloods gang who had participated in this horrible crime was arrested at the Port Authority terminal here in the city. He was charged with kidnapping, robbery and unlawful imprisonment.

I know this story is sickening — there is just no other word for it. But it illustrates the very real dangers that exist on the streets for young runaways at the hands of predators, pushers, pimps, and gangs just like the Bloods.

I want you to know that we constantly warn the

kids here of the incredible dangers that await them in the streets — that the gangs are not their "friends" and never will be.

Sadly, this is not the first time the children we love so much and work so very hard to protect have been brutally victimized by this gang.

In another incident, a young runaway was similarly lured into prostitution by the Bloods gang, robbed of the miserable $140 she made turning two tricks and punched in the face.

Gangs like the Bloods are an ever-present threat to Covenant House, *going so far as to actually infiltrate the safe haven we provide* in an attempt to recruit from within.

But, in spite of our vigilance, events like those I have just described can still take place.

And that convinces me more than ever of the meaning and importance of our work here at Covenant House.

If these horrible dangers did not exist, there would be no need for a place like Covenant House where runaway kids can get a decent meal, a clean warm bed, a listening ear and a loving heart from all of us who devote ourselves to them.

Our work, by its very nature, is difficult, dangerous and, sometimes, very frightening. *But that is exactly why we are here.*

It is also why I need your continued, loving support for the young runaways that can so easily fall victim to the most despicable elements of our society —

criminals, plain and simple — criminals who prey on the young, the innocent, and the needy, for they are such easy prey.

As long as there are kids on the streets who are lonely, hungry and afraid — as long as they remain the prey of vicious sexual predators like the Bloods — we at Covenant House will be there to shelter them, to love them and, I pray, to save them.

And, as long as there are people like you with loving hearts, and generous spirits, I know we will succeed.

Dear Lord,

Thank you for taking care of me.
I never had no one to care about me.
Oh and I'm sorry for what happened
yesterday. Lord, you know why I want
to stay here, because I don't trust
anybody on the streets now. Danger
is always going on. I wish I could
get adopted by a nice person. I've never
been treated nice or like a daughter.
Lord I send wishes for my family
and friends.

> *A prayer written by a kid*
> *in our Covenant House Chapel*

Chapter 8

"His favorite trick was to beat me with a broom handle."

The 180-pound, grey-clad statue sat dead-still in the middle of our shelter, perched atop a large green sofa.

For hours and hours, for many days, the statue just sat there, taking a place amid the bedlam of our shelter, but never taking part in any of it.

Like all statues, the eyes never moved, the hair never went out of place, the body never seemed to move as much as an inch.

But in this case, the statue's eyes were brown, his hair was gold, and his soft, pasty skin hung from his body like an old suit of clothes.

Our statue was a flesh and blood kid named Howie.

He was one of the most unusual homeless kids I've ever met.

He came to us one day like most all our kids do — quietly, tentatively, and unannounced, a lost and lonely kid wandering through life, hoping to find a place to rest his head.

From the moment he stepped inside, we could see that Howie had a little more of a problem talking than most kids. The sounds that came out of his mouth (and there weren't many) were more like grunts than words.

Oftentimes during his first hours here, his mouth would open and remain that way for close to a minute before the sounds began to find their way outside.

Any kind of physical contact, such as a pat on the back or a warm handshake, made him uncomfortable, as if he wasn't ready yet to share any of himself with anyone. It wasn't because he was a bad kid — just a scared one. A very, very scared child....

"We're so glad you found us," we said. No response.

"We want to help you," we said. No response.

"We hope you'll stay and let us be there for you," we said. To this he replied with a grunt.

After we talked to Howie and cleaned him up and fed him and gave him a warm bed to sleep in, we decided to let him find himself in his own way.

For the first few days, he would go down to the center of the shelter, amidst all the bedlam, and then sit transfixed on the couch. On one hand, he desperately wanted to be around people. On the other hand, he desperately didn't know exactly how to interact with us, to reach out, to trust.

He was like a statue in our presence.

As the days wore on, however, and we hovered over him, the words and feelings began to come out. At first, he played tricks, like taking the phone in our shelter off the hook so it would beep and someone would come over and put it back together (that was his way of calling out for attention). Then, finally, he began to speak. The more he spoke, the more we realized why he was so afraid to trust in other people....

"I've been on the street for three months," he said one day, when I came by to say 'hi' and ask how he was feeling.

"I don't have anyplace to go," he said a few minutes later.

"The only place I could go is way too dangerous," he said.

"Do you want to tell me more?" I said. "That sounds like it must have been difficult," I said.

The statue nodded his head, and began to go on. For the first time I could see the beginning of a tear in one of his eyes.

"I lived in a house with my mother, and her boyfriend," he said.

"He used to do some pretty bad stuff to me," he said. "His favorite trick was to beat me with a broom handle," he said.

At that moment he lifted up his shirt slightly, and turned his back toward me so I could see the scars. "It hurt a lot," he said. I touched his back, and patted him on the shoulder for a second, to let him know I cared. "I'm sure that it did," I said softly.

"It got to be where he was beating me every day," he said. "And telling me what a jerk I am. I told my mom about it, but she didn't want to believe me," he said.

"I didn't really have a choice," he said. "I had to get out ... I had to run away ... so I did," he said.

"It wasn't much better out there," he said.

"It was really bad," he said.

Once he began to talk, and find others who would listen and care, the words began to literally pour out.

"I want to make something of my life," he said.

"I want to be somebody," he said.

"Watch me," he said.

One day last week, I picked up my answering machine to hear a familiar voice on the other end. It was Howie, one hour after he had gone for a job interview.

"Hello," a tentative voice said. "I ... I don't know what to say," he said. "I ... did it," he said. "I don't know what else to say," he said. And then the phone clicked off. I could swear I heard a kid crying softly in the background just before the phone clicked off.

I want to thank you for helping Howie. I mean, our kids come to us in all shapes and sizes, from all places, with all kinds of problems. Some of them are so alone and desperate to reach out and connect with someone that they can't stop talking the moment they reach our shelter.

Most of them, however, are more like Howie — so afraid, and insecure and beaten down by reality and the world around them, that it takes a long time to trust enough to share their words with someone else. And it's very, very beautiful when one of these kids makes it. So very beautiful....

Dear Father,

I just want to ask for your help in the time I'm away from my mother and please help me in my actions and my attitude towards people because I know it has got real bad. And Lord please help me in the rest of my teen years because the last five years of my life have been the worst.

I am here Lord to rededicate my life and to comfort my family. I thank you for my life and for the staff members, counselors and Pastors at Covenant House. I need a Bible.

> *A prayer written*
> *by a kid in our*
> *Covenant House Chapel*

Chapter 9

"He seemed to have this thing about my brother," she said.

"I'm afraid to let him out of my sight," the homeless girl said.

"Are you sure he's going to be okay?

"I mean, I think he's really kind of messed up right now ... he needs a lot more help than I do," the homeless girl said. "But he's still my big brother."

Kimberly's eyes welled up and she buried her face in her hands. A minute or two passed quietly and then she raised her head again. There was fire in those tear-filled eyes.

"I know it was probably kind of dumb to run away like we did. I never thought we'd end up with nothing to eat, and no place to go," she said.

"But I had to get him out of there, you know," she said, biting off the word *had* for extra emphasis. "Being in that house was killing him, Sister. I mean, it was killing him."

Her wet eyes looked at me and begged me to understand what she was saying. After just one second looking inside those eyes — and being overwhelmed by her terror, her loneliness, her fear — I knew exactly what she was trying to tell me. I patted her on the shoulder, and cleared my throat.

"So what was going on in that house?" I said. "Was there something bad going on?"

Kimberly sighed, and grimaced, and swallowed

hard. "Oh, yeah," she said softly. "Oh yeah ...

"It was my stepfather," she said. "When he came to live with us, everything was okay for about a year or so. Then he started to really pick on Matty. I don't know why. My brother was only 13.

"Anyway, it got worse and worse, and I kept begging my mother to do something. But she said there was nothing she could do. She said my stepfather was just disciplining Matty.

"And my mom, she had other problems of her own to worry about," she said. "She ... she kind of drank too much. I'm not sure she was even awake half the time when Matty was beaten up.

"It was really awful," she said. The new tears in her eyes said it all ...

"Anyway, my stepfather kept getting worse and worse. He started really beating on Matty. I mean, sometimes he would give Matty two black eyes. I was afraid he was going to kill him.

"I don't know why, but my stepfather never bothered me. He never touched me," she said. "He seemed to have this thing about my brother," she said.

"Finally, he started doing stuff to Matty that was really awful," she said. "I don't want to even tell you," she said. "You can probably guess, though," she said.

"I couldn't take it any more, Sister," she said. "I mean, he's just a kid, and he was crying every night. I couldn't stand to watch it. I tried to tell my mother, but she didn't believe me. She said Matty was lying. But I know he wasn't, Sister," she said. "I know my brother."

"So I decided we had to get out of there. That's why we ran away.

"I don't know what to do now," she said.

"I mean, I think Matty is really hurting," the homeless and all-alone girl said. "He's crying all the time.

"I'll be all right," the homeless girl said.

"But it's him I'm worried about," she said.

"I'm scared for him, and I don't know what to do," she said.

As I looked into Kimberly's eyes, I saw the fierce protectiveness of a loving sister. It was very touching. And very troublesome.

I know she did the right thing to get her brother out of their parents' house. No kid should ever, ever have to suffer from the kind of serious mental, physical and sexual abuse Matty was being subjected to. Ever!

And I do think her brother has some severe emotional problems. We're going to get him professional help immediately.

But as I talked to Kimberly, I also worried about her.

What an amazing kid. What a powerful love. She risked everything — she even risked her own life because she knew her brother was being destroyed.

I wonder how she will come through all this. She has taken on an awful lot of responsibility for a kid her age. That's why I'm praying for her as well as her brother. And I am determined to do everything we can to help Kimberly. She needs a safe place to live. She needs a chance to finish school.

She needs to stay close to her brother.

Dear Lord,

*I believe in you but I am so confused
about where I'm going — all I know
is where I've been. I am so scared
and I have no one to talk to but myself
and I hide my feelings in my music.*

> *A prayer written
> by a kid in our
> Covenant House Chapel*

Chapter 10

"I want to be a somebody, some day," she said.

"I don't know if I should show you this," she said, biting her lip.

"It's kind of personal," she said, biting harder.

"Please don't laugh at me," she said.

She leaned down and rummaged her hands through the back side of the bottom dresser drawer in her bedroom. Slowly, gently, ever-so-meticulously, she began to pull spiral notebooks out of the drawer — first one, then two, then three, until she had pulled out six notebooks in all.

She faced me again, six notebooks stacked precariously in her arms, and she began to open her mouth to talk to me, but the words were barely able to trickle out. "Here's the first one," she said, handing me the top notebook, in a whisper so soft I could barely make out her words. "And the second," she whispered on, "and the third." Soon, I was standing in front of her with ten pounds of lined paper in my arms, and a hundred questions racing through my head.

The tears which began to fill her eyes told me that I had been entrusted with something no one else had ever seen before.

I cleared my throat, and smiled my thanks.

"These look very important," I said.

"Thank you for letting me see them," I said.

"Could you and I look at them together?" I said.

I spoke to her, not knowing what was inside the

books, but knowing I had to find out. "Thanks," her eyes said. "That would be nice," they said. "But please ... I hope you won't laugh at me," her eyes said.

"Do you want to look at this one first?" I asked, taking the top notebook from the pile.

"No," she said, reaching out her hands, and grabbing the bottom book in the stack. The book had a big number one on the front cover. "This is where it all kind of started," she said.

"I started writing about two years ago," she said. "When I was still out on the street. I didn't have any friends ... I didn't have anyone to talk to ... I thought I was going to burst ... so I just started writing," she said, almost apologetically.

"The stuff inside here is pretty tough," she said.

I opened the pages and began to turn them slowly, reading the words as quickly as I could. The pages were creased and folded and smudged. The words that filled each page were almost like artwork, they were sketched so beautifully and carefully. The content ... the content hurt a lot to read.

> *"I am so alone, so desperate, so lonely," one passage began on page four. "Why have I ended up like this? What have I done wrong? Help me understand, God — why doesn't anyone love me?"*

Another passage near the end of the first notebook spoke of her desperation and her pain ...

> *"It's been two months now since I ran away from the abuse that was killing me at 'home.' I wonder what it must be like for other kids who never have to run away? What must it be like*

*to spend a night in a warm bed, safe and
secure? I would give anything not to be sleeping in a subway tonight. Anything ..."*

I put the first notebook down and told her how
much I felt the pain she was feeling when she wrote
each word. Shelia's life had not been easy ...

She had come to us two months ago, a scared and
scarred and alone and urgently desperate kid.

"My father used to do awful things to me," she told
me that first night.

"He ... he used to beat me a lot," she said. "And
other stuff," she said.

"I was scared he was going to kill me ... I thought
I was going to die," she told me.

Terrified of dying at home, Shelia fled to the street,
searching for a better life. Instead, she found what
almost all kids find on the street — a lonely, sometimes
very dark world, filled with pimps and pushers and
pornographers who make a livelihood out of feeding
off scared kids like Shelia.

What this world can do to an innocent kid is heartbreaking to see. Inevitably, kids like Shelia find themselves turning inward, actively wondering whether they
are to blame for what has happened to them.

"Maybe I am bad," these kids begin to say to themselves. "Maybe I do deserve to be abused, maybe I do
deserve to be unloved, maybe I do deserve to die on the
street." Can you imagine being a teenage kid, and feeling that kind of self-doubt and pain?

I look at Shelia, and she looked back and tried to
smile. I think she knew what I was thinking about, and
how much I was probably hurting for her inside. I

smiled, and told her how proud I was of her again.

"Here," she said. "I think you'll like this." And then she handed me a book marked with a big "4" on the outside.

"This is when things get better," she said. "Here, start here," she said, pointing to a page midway through the notebook.

I looked down at the page. It was filled with big 'exclamation marks' at the top and hearts. "Why don't you read this part out loud," she said …

> *"I did it today," it began. "I finally decided to go to this place some other street kids were telling me about, Covenant House. I don't know exactly what it is about this place, but for the first time in a long time, I feel a little at peace, even hopeful. Everyone here is so nice — they've given me food, and they told me I was welcome, and they've let me pick out some clean clothes.*
>
> *"And tonight, I'm actually going to sleep on a clean bed, for the first time in … I forget how long it's been. I kind of feel like crying tonight. I'm so happy, but I don't think it's going to last. The good things in life never do …"*

I looked over at Shelia, and I could see the tears beginning to run down her face. The memory of that moment — the feelings of hope, desperation, contentment, fear — came back to her, as if it happened yesterday.

It was maybe the single most important moment of her life.

"That was beautiful, Shelia," I said. "May I go on?"

She paused for a moment, a million thoughts racing through her head. "I think the next couple of notebooks are pretty private," she said. "I mean, most of the pages are filled with really nice stuff, about the time I've been here at Covenant House, and all the things I've learned, and done, but I'm not sure you have to see all that," she said, half apologetically.

"But maybe you could just take a look at this one," she said, handing me the last notebook.

"What's inside?" I asked.

"Oh, some other kinds of things I've done," she said.

"I want to be a writer some day," she said.

I opened the last notebook, and began to read. The pages were crammed with things Shelia had written ... poems, notes to herself, short stories. She had even tried her hand at writing an episode for a television show. Her passion and her gift for writing literally screamed from the pages. She is a very, very talented young woman ...

"I love to write," she said, after I had told her how wonderful the notebook was. "I want to do that for a living," she said. "I want to be a somebody, some day," she said.

"You already are," I said. "Don't ever forget that," I said. "I'm very, very proud of you, and very impressed," I said.

"Thanks," she said very softly, barely able to get out the words. "That means a lot," she said.

We spoke for a few more minutes, Shelia and I. The passion she has for things — her passion for life, her passion for writing, her passionate thanks for the chance we've given her — poured out of her as she spoke. Her happiness and zest for living gave me goosebumps.

*God, please don't let me walk
the road alone, or I think I will die.
I need help in this troubled world.
Please help me and others in
my position because it's hard
mentally and physically. Thank
you for providing me with a safe
place to stay. I thank you Lord
for helping me through the day.*

*Written by a
Covenant House kid*

Chapter 11

"I was afraid he'd kill me."

"I know that people can tell when they look at me.

"I'm sure they know what happened to me.

"I can feel them looking down on me.

"I can see it in their eyes, Sister.

"People treat me like I'm dirty ... like they don't want to be around me.

"I think they all know what happened to me ..."

He shrugged his shoulders and ran his hands through his hair, and then ran them across his shirt in order to dry them. I call Chris "the clean kid" because he's always — and I mean always — in the shower, washing himself.

If you were to visit our shelter tomorrow (and by the way, the invitation is always there!) and met Chris, you'd be able to pick him out pretty easily. He's the freshly scrubbed kid with the always-damp hair, who looks down at the ground a lot because he's afraid of what others are saying about him.

To most people, he's a really nice looking kid. But all Chris sees inside himself is filth ... filth he can't seem to escape ...

When you hear his story, you'll understand why....

"It all began with my stepfather when I was about thirteen," he said.

"I mean, I can remember that first time like it was

yesterday," he said.

"My mom was out for awhile, and my stepfather was really drunk, and he started doing stuff to me. I tried fighting him, but he told me he'd kill me if I ever said anything."

"After that, I thought maybe it wouldn't happen again. But a couple months later, my stepfather came in to my room again when no one else was home.

"It went on like that, off and on, for years.

"I finally couldn't take it anymore. I told my mom, but she got real mad at me, and didn't believe me.

"I finally had no choice. I wrote my mom a note and told her I loved her, but I couldn't stay anymore. And I just ran....

"I didn't know where I was running to, I just had to get away. I didn't want my stepfather to find me ... I was afraid he'd kill me.

"So, I hopped on a bus, and headed to New York. I didn't know what else to do ..."

He told his story slowly, but without much emotion, a mixture of flat syllables punctuated by heavy sighs. I know there was a lot more of the story to be told, about life on the street, and the agony and loneliness and terror he encountered, and the systematic dismantling of whatever hope and dignity he once had. But he didn't even want to re-live that part right now ... as bad as street life was for him, *it wasn't even the worst chapter* in his life.

He still desperately, achingly needed to come to

terms with what came before that. And so far he wasn't succeeding ...

"I'm so sorry about what happened to you, Chris," I said.

"I think you're a really good kid ... I know you're a really good kid," I said.

"And when I look at you, that's exactly what I see ... a very nice, polite, good boy, who'd I'd be very proud to have as a son," I said.

"I'm sure that's what every one else sees, too," I said.

He looked at me, and the tears began to fill his eyes, and I could tell how much my words meant to him. Like a lot of our kids, he was starving — literally starving — to hear something good about himself. Something that told him he was decent, and worthy, and good.

Something they had never heard someone say to them before.

"Thanks, Sister," he said softly. "I'm glad someone sees that," he says.

"That's what everyone sees in you, Chris," I said.

He didn't answer. I think he may have been too choked up to say anything. But the tears streaming down his face told me he heard what I had said.

"I think I might go outside for a while," he said. "Take a walk outside," he said. "It's been a while," he said.

"That sounds good," I said. "I'll see you later at dinner," I said. "Take care of yourself."

He sighed, and mumbled another soft 'thanks,' and headed off to the door. "I'll see you later, right?" I said.

"That'd be good," he said. "Maybe we can talk some more," he said.

"I'd like that," I said.

I smiled and whispered a quiet thank you to God. I think he's going to make it. Thank you for helping me be there for him....

No stranger I, to death.
He lives with me each day.
He tempts me with my grave,
and hides the price I'll pay.

A poem from a street kid

Chapter 12

"As he walked off into the darkness, we wondered if we'd ever see him again."

He came to our van last night, an 18-year-old ghost of a kid, walking his last days on this earth.

In his trembling left hand he held a spiral bound notepad, in his right a tattered history book. The worn shirt on his back was the same one he had on for months, except time had taken its toll.

"Do you think you could hold these books for me awhile," he said, as he does every time we see him. "I'll be back in a couple hours, maybe you could just keep these for me while I'm gone," he said.

"Do you have to leave so soon," we said, while handing him a baloney sandwich, and some fruit punch in a plastic cup.

"Yeah, I'm afraid I do," he said in the weary and tired voice of an older man. "I gotta lot of work to do tonight. My mom really needs me right now … it's just her and my two little sisters, and she's pretty sick still," he said. "Her bills are stacking pretty high these days," he said.

"I'll be back for the books in a while."

With that he gave us a tired wave, and turned off into the darkness to begin another night's work.

We call him the dirty blond haired kid, because he's too embarrassed after all these months to tell us his name.

And his job is something no kids should ever be forced to do … working the nightshift on the streets, as a professional prostitute.

When our van workers first met him way back when, he was much different … a kid. A kids' smile and innocence. A kid's energy and vitality. A kid's mind and body and soul and spirit. But that was 'back then.'

"I gotta find a way to earn some money for my mom," he told us way back then. "She can't work any more, and she really needs my help.

"I'm not sure what I'm going to do, but I got some ideas," he said. "She'd be really mad at me if she found out about it though," he said.

The tears in his eyes and the fear in his voice told us what his "ideas" were. His body language made it clear that what he was about to do made him want to vomit.

"Come stay with us," we said. "We can help you," we said.

"Nah … wish I could," he said. "I gotta do this," he said. "But thanks," he said.

As time went on, and he slipped into the life of a prostitute, our little friend changed right before our eyes.

His bright and energetic eyes slowly grew colder. The stride in his step stiffened. His body and demeanor became courser … grungier.

Like so many kids thrown to the wolves on the street, he became what's commonly known as 'rough trade". Worn. Tired. A used-up, beaten-up, abused and over-the-hill commodity.

From time to time, whenever we saw him, we held out hope we could reel him in, and save what was left of his life.

I mean, this kid is a very special kid ... with a zest and passion for reading and learning unlike anything I've ever seen in my life.

If you had ridden in our van any night and run into the dirty blond haired kid with us, chances are you'd have seen him holding a couple books – usually history texts borrowed from other kids at school, or novels. Sometimes our outreach van glove compartment contained three paperbacks that belonged to him. He was never, ever without a book in his hands...

"You're incredibly bright," we often said to him. "Come with us," we said. "We can help you get into college," we said.

"I'd love that," he said, letting his mind and heart drift to a faraway dream. "But I can't.

"I mean, can you help me feed my brother and sister," he'd reply. "Can you help me feed my mother? Can you pay her rent?"

And then he would drift off into the night, a worn and tattered boy, doing whatever he could to keep his family alive.

It's harder every time we see him not to get angry at what life has done to him...

"Come back with us," we said when we saw him last night. "Let us help you get off the streets," we said.

"I can't," he said. "It's too late for me," he said. "That's ok, though," he said.

"Don't worry about it, though, ok?" he said. "I mean, it isn't too bad," he said.

"I'll be alright," he said. "No big deal," he said. "Hey, could you hold this book for me," he said.

"Maybe I'll see you later," he said. It was less a statement, than a question.

As he walked off into the darkness, we wondered if we'd ever see his face again.

Please ... could you say a prayer tonight for this beautiful child? Will you join me in asking God to watch over him a little extra tonight, to keep him safe, and most of all to guide him back to our outreach van, so perhaps we can finally get him the help he desperately needs? Please, do that if you can. Thank you.

"On the street I saw a girl
cold and shivering in a thin
dress, with little hope of a
decent meal. I became angry
and said to God: 'Why did
you permit this? Why don't
you do something about it?'
For a while God said nothing.
That night He replied quite
suddenly: 'I certainly did
something about it.
I made you.'"

Chapter 13

"It's hopeless ... I'm hopeless."

"I was born to be an addict, Sister," he said.

"And I'm going to die an addict too," he said.

"It's in my blood, Sister," he said. "I'm a hopeless case. I don't think you should waste your time on me anymore," he said.

He shuffled his feet, and he stared into my eyes, and he lifted his shoulders slowly and made a gentle shrug.

I could almost hear the bones rattle under his clothes when he moved. Everything about him — his dirty hair, his hollow eyes, his pale skin, his tattered clothes — seemed tired and lifeless and old. He was breathing air in and out, but he wasn't really living anymore. He was a kid just marking time until he turned the page on the last chapter of his life.

His story didn't look like it had much longer to go....

"I know things don't seem that good right now, Freddy," I said. "But there's always hope."

"I know you can make it," I said.

He smiled softly, and crinkled his eyes and shook his head slowly as my final words drifted out.

"I wish I could believe that," he said.

"I used to, you know," he said.

"But that was a long, long time ago.

"I'm not trying to be a wise guy, or anything Sister," he said. "I'd give anything in the world to not be an addict.

"But I can't beat this thing. I've been through treatment lots of times already," he said.

"It's hopeless ... I'm hopeless ... *it's just in my blood."*

He shrugged his shoulders again, as tears began to form in the corners of his eyes and drop down his face. I felt so powerless at that moment, watching him stand there, drowning in his desperation, waiting for a death he felt was inevitable.

Nothing about his life had ever been easy.

He had been born seventeen years ago in one of those small old mill towns in the Northeast, the kind of town where industry and hope left town and never looked back at what was left behind. Unable to find work, unable to cope, his parents both took to drinking as a way to escape their sorrow.

Sometimes, when the drink wasn't enough to ease their pain, they took their frustrations out on Freddy. Many nights, Freddy found himself hiding in his house, in closets and under beds, trying to escape a beating that had, by that point, become an almost weekly ritual.

Afraid, and desperate to please his parents, Freddy began drinking with them, in order to show he was on their side. Soon, well before he had become a teen-ager, he found himself hooked on alcohol, unable to pry himself loose from the grip it had on him.

> *"It's in my blood Sister," he said to us that
> first day. "I was born an addict ... there's
> nothing you can do to help me."*

One day, when the beatings got to be too much, he fled to the streets to find a peace he had never known.

Instead, he found what all kids find — the aloneness, hunger, fatigue and darkness of an unforgiving world on the street.

He was sixteen years old.

For one full year, Freddy struggled to find some kind of existence on the streets. He slept in alleys, and ate out of garbage cans. He drank to forget how scared and alone he was — and he began experimenting with drugs, hoping they would somehow help him escape his pain. He died a little, day by day.

Then he found Covenant House.

I'm not sure exactly how it's going to turn out for him. I'm hoping — I guess some would say against hope — that it's not too late to reach him, that it's not too late for him to believe, that it's not too late for him to finally overcome an addiction that has an ironclad grip on every ounce of his body.

I do know that as long as he is alive, I have hope that we can turn his life around. And as long as we have friends like you, we will have the means to make that lifesaving turnaround possible. (I can't thank you enough for that, you literally do make the difference between life and death for these kids.)

"I want you to know something, Freddy," I said.

"I still think you are going to make it," I said.

"Just give us the chance," I said.

I could tell by the look in his eyes that he hoped I was right. "I'd like to try," he said. I reached out and hugged him. "Thank you, God," I whispered to myself.

That was three months ago. I must admit, I wasn't super hopeful that we could help — he was in such bad shape.

But now, I've got incredible, wonderful news! Freddy's turnaround has been remarkable! Ever since that first night I met Freddy, we've been watching over him like a whole flock of mother hens. He went through a drug and alcohol addiction program and really worked hard. It wasn't easy for him. He went through hell. But he kept going.

Now he is feeling good. He no longer believes he is destined to die on the streets. He has an important job working for a company that cleans up hazardous waste. He takes it very seriously and just got a special license.

He has put on weight. I hardly recognize him. The transformation has been just remarkable.

Not every kid turns around this dramatically. You know that. But sometimes, what you give kids like Freddy truly is miraculous. The "before" and "after" pictures of this kid are a tribute to your love and care. (Of course, three months of sobriety is only a "beginning" for someone battling this kind of addiction. He's still got a long way to go — and we're going to work with him to make sure he stays totally connected to a support system that can help him stay on the right path. It won't be easy for him, but … I really feel he's going to make it!)

Thank you for helping Freddy. Thank you for helping me show him that he is not hopeless. Thank you for helping us show him that God loves him. I thank God for you every day.

*"The love of God is
creative to infinity."*

St. Vincent de Paul

Chapter 14

"I finally decided that I couldn't take it anymore."

"You don't think God punished me by taking my leg, do you, Sister?"

Julie had that anxious, hopeful look that I see so often from kids who want desperately for someone to tell them that the terrible things that have happened to them are not their fault.

"No, Julie," I said. "God doesn't do that. I'm quite sure of that."

Julie raised her eyebrows just a bit and then relaxed.

"You're right, Sister. I hope you're right.

"It's just that so many things have happened to me that sometimes I think I must have done something wrong.

"I never knew my mother. No one knows where she is. I lived with my grandmother until I was 10. Until then, my life was okay. Except for the pains in my leg. It hurt for a long time, but the doctors couldn't find anything wrong.

"Then, when I was 10, my grandmother died. She was 84 years old."

Julie stopped and her eyes filled with tears. She frowned and sighed. "I really miss her.

"At first, I was excited to be going to live with my

father. I had only met him a couple times, but he was my father, my DAD, you know what I mean. I day-dreamed all the time about how great life was going to be with my DAD."

Julie stopped again, and this time the tears flowed.

"But it didn't turn out that way. The second night I was there, he started abusing me, you know, doing things to me. I was only 10 years old and I didn't know what to do.

"In my daydreams, my father always loved me.

"Then, a year later, the pains in my leg got so bad that the doctor did some more tests and found out I had bone cancer. So they amputated my leg below the knee.

"They also took me away from my father and put me in a foster home. That didn't work out so good, so I got moved to another foster home.

"And then I was moved again.

"And again.

"And again.

"Four times I was moved," she sighed, barely a whisper now. "It was pretty tough," she said.

"Then one day, I finally decided that I couldn't take it anymore," she said. "I was tired of people taking me in and then saying I couldn't stay," she said.

"I finally decided to run away. I had to. I mean, Sister, can you imagine what that was like?" she said.

She stood there and blinked her eyes, and grew very quiet, as I patted her shoulder and told her how sorry I was for her. As she stood in our shelter, tears streaming down her face, I could see her heart and mind flee in a thousand different directions.

I know where they were going wasn't very pleasant, an endless journey of dead end streets in strange places, where the days and nights always ended up being dark, and unforgiving, and excruciatingly lonely.

It wasn't hard to see the questions pounding inside her head either (it was very painful to see those questions, but it wasn't very hard....) *"Why me?"* her heart kept asking, again and again. *"What is it about me, that this is happening?*

"Why doesn't anyone care about me?" I could see her heart asking. *"Why doesn't anyone love me? Will anyone ever love me?"*

As she stood there, and the questions kept pounding in her head, she began to bend slowly at the waist, and reach her right hand down to her artificial leg. I'm pretty sure she didn't even realize she was drumming her fingers against her leg at that moment. I guess it was just something she did subconsciously, something that helped her remind herself of the way her life had turned, and the losses she had felt.

As painful as losing that leg had been (and I can't imagine that happening to me when I was a teenager), I think it paled in comparison to the losses she felt inside her heart.

I pulled her close to me for a second, and hugged her. She stepped back, and tried to smile a brave smile, but she wasn't very good at pulling it off.

"I guess that's why I wonder if God is punishing

me," she said. "I mean, the doctor just told me that my cancer has returned. He wants to amputate further, up to my thigh. He says I need chemotherapy, too.

"But I can't do that either, even if it kills me," she said.

"I mean, I have someone else to worry about now, too," she said.

"I mean, I have to worry about my baby now, too," she said, lightly patting her stomach.

Like so many young girls, whose teenage lives are filled with one day of rejection after another, Julie had looked for love when she ran to the streets.

"I know I should have waited," she said. "I made a dumb mistake," she said. "But he said he loved me," she said. "He said he wanted to have a family," she said.

"I should have known he was lying," she said.

I looked at her and smiled and told her I understood. I thought for a second Julie would begin to cry again, but instead something else began to overtake her. Something wonderful, and heroic and beautiful ...

It was then, at that moment, that Julie brightened for the first time that day. Her eyes sparkled. "The thing is, I really want to have this baby. I know I should have waited, but it's too late for that. And I love this baby already.

"I want to be like my grandmother. I want to give this baby a happy childhood. I really do.

"So I told them to hold off on the chemo. Till after the baby is born. They tell me I'm risking my life, but

I want my baby to be healthy. I'll take my chances.

"Things will work out. I'm sure of it. I've been praying a lot, and I'm sure things are going to work out."

One of the hardest things about working at Covenant House is living with the knowledge that sometimes things don't work out. I couldn't bring myself to tell Julie that. I said, "Julie, I'll be praying for you, too. We all will."

So I am praying for Julie today. I'm going to pray for her a lot over the next few months until the baby is born and Julie is able to resume cancer treatments.

I really hope we can save her. She is such a beautiful kid. So brave in the face of so much pain — physical and emotional.

The most remarkable thing about her is that, despite all that she's been through, she is one of the most cheerful people I know. Always smiling. Always laughing.

It's impossible not to love her.

"I bound myself by oath,
I made a covenant with you ...
and you became mine."

Ezekiel 16:8

*(Our oath, the first thing
kids see when they walk
into our shelter.)*

Faith Into Action

*Your invitation to join the Covenant House
Faith Community*

By now you know that Covenant House is more than a shelter for kids – it's a mission inspired by, ed by and dedicated to God. For some very special people, just reading about our kids is not enough. They want to be part of this work, to see firsthand what our kids go through.

It's for these people that the Covenant House Faith Community was created.

The extraordinary people of our Faith Community come from all walks of life, from every corner of the country. They are as young as 21 and as old as their mid-70's. But as different as they are, they all share a common purpose – to leave our kids' world, and all our worlds, a better place than they found it. Community members live together in prayer and service to God and to the kids of Covenant House. This commitment to homeless kids is a true expression of the gospel and an enriching experience for our members.

Listen to Joan Conroy, a Faith Community Member from March 2003 through October 2005, as she shares what Faith Community meant to her...

I didn't know...

I didn't know how powerful unconditional love was, and that I'd be able to offer and receive it from so many of our kids. I didn't know that living in community would force me to examine myself so much. I didn't know how to break up a fight. I didn't know the hundreds of ways you could measure success. I didn't know that I would never learn it all or see it all. I didn't know how many times my heart would break from the stories I heard of our kids' lives. I didn't know how much being a part of Faith Community would touch and inspire those around me. I didn't expect all the laughter, jokes, and smiles. I didn't know the power of remembering a name, or of being a familiar face. I didn't know that I would lie awake at night worrying about our kids. I didn't realize how much my heart could break for another's pain. I didn't know how many kids were survivors. I didn't know how to write a progress note, or do an assessment. I didn't know the empowerment of choice. I didn't know that I'd learn about self-lessness from a bunch of teenagers. I didn't know what to do if someone's water broke. I didn't know how many times I would pray, "God be with me." I didn't know I'd laugh so much, learn so much, and love so much. I didn't know that in serving our kids, I would give more than I had, and receive so much more than I gave.

Come learn with us ... come share your gifts ... come help us transform the lives of some brave, beautiful, tough, loving kids. For more information or an application to Faith Community, visit our website at www.CovenantHouse.org/FaithCommunity.

Epilogue

In 1972 in Times Square a simple, profound mission began ... a mission to rescue homeless kids from the street. Today Covenant House is the most powerful human rights movement for children in the world. And it begins and ends with love.

"Covenant" means a lot of different things to a lot of different people. To me, it means God's promise and love for His children will always be fulfilled. The staff, volunteers, and supporters of Covenant House are the people called to fulfill that promise, every hour of every day. And in return, we are blessed with the greatest opportunity of all – the chance to help the brave, good kids who come to us for help.

Recently I spoke with the first child I ever worked with at Covenant House back in 1992. She is now a mom of four and a nurse, but back then she was a kid who was as broken and empty as anyone you could ever meet. Covenant House was the bridge from her brokenness to healing.

As I pulled together the stories for this humble book, I was struck by the courage, the resiliency, and the goodness of our kids. I consider it the greatest, most profound blessing of my life to be a part of this mission and a part of the healing that takes place in our programs around the country and throughout Latin America and Canada.

The challenges we face are great. Simply stated, the number of street kids is growing. This year, more than 1,000,000 kids will end up on America's streets.

As the pages of this book too readily illustrate, we have always had street kids. But in today's America, an America continually beset by family units breaking down and breaking up, neighborhoods falling apart, and community clubs and associations deteriorating – the numbers of kids falling by the wayside is a national crisis.

Even worse, while the number of new kids pouring out onto our streets is increasing, the criminals who buy and sell vulnerable kids are more organized and ruthless than ever before.

The sex industry has rapidly expanded over the past several decades and requires a dramatically amplified effort. More than one million of the world's children are trafficked for labor or sexual exploitation each year, robbed of their childhoods and forced into slavery and brutality. Here in the United States, as many as 20,000 kids are trafficked *within our borders* each year.

Last year Covenant House served more than 70,000 homeless kids in 16 U.S. cities, and many of them had been solicited on the streets or muscled into the sex trade. Time and time again, we see sex traffickers target children because of their vulnerability and gullibility, as well as the twisted market demand for young victims.

And it's what we *don't see* that should worry us all. The sex for sale industry in this country used to be a lot more public, and a lot more vulnerable. Back when Covenant House was first born, teenage prostitutes were forced to roam the streets to ply their trade, and it was easier for them to flee to our shelter doors. Now however, most sexual liaisons are planned via cell phones or over the internet, so the entire gruesome process – the set-up, the liaison, the follow-up – is all conducted behind closed doors. Out of sight. And in far too many instances, out of our reach.

We must wake up to the growing number of homeless and abandoned kids on our streets. Alone and isolated, many times disconnected from family and friends, these kids are desperate for alternatives to the streets. On their behalf, I offer an urgent call to service: We simply must reignite, state by state, street outreach efforts by schools, civic groups, police, human service agencies and child advocates to bring our kids into safety before they are solicited or kidnapped by the pimps and gangs who steal their childhoods for profit, then throw them away.

More than ever, the race to rescue these kids is a race against the clock. Every day, every hour.

I pray this book will prevent children from running away and will involve more people – people like you – in being part of the solutions to the grave problems our kids face.

Jesus' directive to us that "what you do to the least of My children, you do to Me" is lived out every day and in every kid who comes to us at Covenant House. May He give us the wisdom to recognize every young person as a special child of God, and the strength to give all our kids the love and respect they so desperately need.

> **Kevin M. Ryan, President**
> **Covenant House**

Where do we go from here?

My newsletters tell an incredible story ... but they only tell part of the story. Wrapped around the letters I wrote to my friends, I've also included words written to me by others — poems and prayers written by our kids.

And almost every word in this book — whether they were penned by me, a runaway kid, or a teenager in school — carries a consistent message: the American family is falling apart. And we must, each of us, do what we can to repair it. Now!

I passionately believe the breakdown of the family unit is the single deepest ethical and moral challenge of our generation. Whether we respond to it will depend on the resolve and willingness of all of us to commit ourselves to the care and protection of family life. The time for repairing endangered families and rescuing their children is not after they have fallen apart!

The question then is ... how? How can each of us make a difference in repairing the American family? And how can we begin to make that difference now?

Because the survival of the family is so very important to our futures, we have prepared a special Family Survival Guide which can be found on the following pages. This Guide features the best things we've learned over the years working with hundreds of thousands of kids, as well as good, time-tested values that we never let ourselves forget. We hope you will share these pages with a parent you know who may need help. Thank you!

Family Survival Guide

*Reflections on
Raising Kids Today*

Values — Teaching Them in Today's World.

Communicating your values has never been more important than it is today. And the good news is, it all begins and ends with you.

When all is said and done, parents have far more influence over instilling values in their kids than any other factor.

Here are some simple, and very important, things we should all remember about values, and passing them along:

- Kids get their sense of what's right and wrong from people they love and respect. No one has more influence over teaching values than you do. Your input can make all the difference!

- When it comes to teaching values .... action *always* speak louder than words. Kids today have a "show me" mentality. They need to see the values lived out by you. Respect for life, respect for other people, honesty, integrity ... kids get those from watching you. The old saw has never been more true ... children *do* learn what they live!

- Families are still the best vehicle for raising children. A loving, nurturing family unit, of whatever form, creates the kind of environment kids need to learn what's right and wrong ... and how to love themselves too. Values are best inculcated in an environment of love and acceptance.

- Always take time to sit and talk to your kids. Don't be afraid to say what you feel (but don't ever be too closed to listen to what your kids think).

- Always strive to teach your kids to love and respect themselves as children of God. A healthy love and respect for themselves is incredibly important for any kid. It's also the first essential step in helping a kid also learn a love and respect for those around him, and God.

- Nobody has said it better than Jesus. Those three words, "Love Thy Neighbor...." are an important message for every kid!

You've Got a Tough Job.

Most of us were never taught to be parents. So we can't help but disappoint ourselves sometimes. How often have you heard yourself using the very words you hated hearing from your own parents?

And when our kids become teenagers, it gets even harder. They seem to reject everything we've taught them. As far as they're concerned, we know nothing. Our values and beliefs are constantly challenged. Every word we utter is seen as interference. Emotions run high.

But we're more important to our teens than ever. As they try out the values of their peers, who are more influential than ever, we counter the pull of drugs and alcohol. These entangle children every day and can ruin their lives.

The Stakes are High.

Teenagers who don't get what they need at home look elsewhere. Some run away from home. Many more consider other ways of running from pressure — a once bright and happy son escapes to drugs, a vivacious daughter starts drinking. Think about these facts:

- Each year, one million students drop out of high school or are chronically truant.
- Four out of 10 teenage girls will become pregnant before age 20.
- Although marijuana use has declined in the past years, addiction to cocaine, especially crack, has doubled.
- One in four teens develops a drinking problem during his teen years; about 10,000 will die in alcohol-related accidents this year.
- Each year, 5,000 to 6,000 teens die in suicide-related deaths, and the number is growing, one every 90 minutes. For every death, at least 100 other young people attempt suicide.

The Turbulent Teens.

Teens face many pressures that adults don't take seriously. Their bodies are changing — they have to adjust to the new person they see in the mirror. They feel different. They become interested in sex.

Self-doubt is constant. They feel pressure to conform and fear ridicule if they don't.

These changes can be bewildering, frightening and even depressing.

Teens can have remarkable insights. But they also surprise us with their lack of good judgment.

Your Teen Needs You.

At the time teenagers are crying out to be treated as adults, they also need a nurturing home, a refuge. And though they deny it passionately, they need structure, limits, lots of help sorting out their lives and, most important, love.

In the turbulence of growing up, it is important for us parents to remember (even if our teens seem to forget) that we love each other. In the end, that's what makes the whole struggle worthwhile.

How Well Do You Know Your Kids?

You may say, "My teenager wouldn't do that." Most don't. But even if yours wouldn't, think about the following questions:

- Where is your child right now?
- What are your teen's deepest fears?
- Who is your son or daughter's best friend?
- Do your teen's friends feel welcome in your home?

Remember, a strong relationship with your children is the best way for you to guide them, and to prevent them from becoming a sorry statistic.

Getting Along With Your Teen.

Here are some ideas and techniques you can try to improve your relationship with your teen. If they don't work at first, keep trying. They take practice.

1. Make time for your teen. Find an activity you enjoy doing together and pursue it. If your invitations are declined, keep asking.

2. Listen, really listen. Because parents have so much to do and so little time, we often try to listen while cleaning, washing dishes or fixing the car. Put your chores aside so your teen knows you're really paying attention.

3. Take the long view. Don't treat minor mishaps as major catastrophes. Choose the important issues. Don't make your home a battleground.

4. Tolerate differences. View your teenager as an individual distinct from you. This doesn't mean you can't state your opinion if you disagree.

5. Respect your teenager's privacy. If a behavior is worrying you, speak up.

6. Let your teens sort things out themselves. Never say that you know how your teen feels. They believe their feelings (so new and personal) are unique. They'll learn otherwise — without your help. And never imply that their feelings don't matter or will change. Because teens live in the present, it doesn't matter that they'll soon feel differently.

7. Don't judge. State facts instead of opinions when

you praise or criticize. Stating facts like "Your poem made me smile," or "This report card is all Cs and Ds!" leaves it up to your teen to draw the appropriate conclusions. Teens are sensitive about being judged — positively as well as negatively.

8. Be generous with praise. Praise your child's efforts, not just accomplishments. And don't comment on the person. "You're a great artist" is hard to live up to. "I loved that drawing" is a fact and comes from your heart.

9. Set reasonable limits. Teens need them. Your rules should be consistently applied — and rooted in your deepest beliefs and values.

10. Teach your teen to make sensible decisions and choices by encouraging independence and letting your teenager make mistakes. Don't step in unless you have to.

How to Make Anger Work.

All parents get furious at their children. We can't help it. But some parents feel bad about being angry and keep quiet. Though it's easy to say things in anger that you don't mean, anger can also spark talks that will help you and your teen get to know each other better.

Some Guidelines.

• When you get mad, don't blame or accuse. Say how you *feel* — annoyed, irritated, upset, etc. —

and why. Be specific. Talk facts. Blaming only forces a teen to argue his point, arouses tempers, and kills dialogue.

- Think solution, not victory. Don't try to win arguments.
- Stick to the present incident. Fighting old battles will only aggravate a situation.
- Be careful not to attack your teen's person or character. Say, "I'm furious that you didn't clean up after the mess you made" — *not*, "You're a lazy slob!" Your son or daughter may give up trying to improve.
- If the situation is touchy, put your ideas in a letter. You can say exactly what you mean — and your teen will have time to think it over before answering.

Signs That Your Child Needs Outside Help.

- Suicidal talk of any kind. A suicidal teen may also give away valued possessions, make a will, talk about death or dying or say his family would be better off without him.
- Recent changes in sleeping or eating habits, thinking patterns, personality, friendships, study habits, activities. A sudden unexplained end to a long depression often precedes a suicide attempt. Major weight loss can be a sign of bulimia or anorexia — dangerous problems.
- Drug or alcohol use. You might notice: irrational

or irresponsible behavior, lying, secretiveness, severe mood swings, a sudden increase in accidents. A teen with a problem may have dilated pupils or wear sunglasses indoors, or complain about not sleeping or not feeling well. Valuables may disappear. You may find drug paraphernalia or alcohol containers around the house.

- A recent change in friends who you feel may be involved with drugs or alcohol may indicate that your child is involved or be a sign that your child is having other problems.

- Law-breaking behavior, even if the police and courts aren't involved. You might notice new possessions and money not accounted for.

- Poor self-image. Doubts are normal. But persistently low self-esteem is a problem.

- Serious depression. Listlessness, loneliness, withdrawal, difficulty making friends.

- Rebelliousness to the point of total, continual defiance.

- Problems at school, including class-cutting, absenteeism, a sudden drop in grades.

- Fears or anxieties that interfere with everyday activities.

- Problems between family members that aren't solved by listening and discussing. In fact, family changes such as a death, divorce or remarriage are times when teens often need some outside help.

When to Get Help for Yourself.

- Things aren't going well with your family but you can't figure out why.
- You disagree totally with positions your spouse has taken on issues concerning your teen and the two of you can't find a compromise.
- You have trouble holding a job.
- You are abusing drugs or alcohol.
- You get violent with your teenager and can't control yourself.
- Your spouse gets violent with you or your child.

What to Do if Your Teen Runs Away.

Most kids who run away return within 48 hours. Those who stay away can find themselves in many dangerous situations. So do everything you can to bring your child home.

- Keep a notebook recording steps you've taken and dates.
- Check in with: neighbors, relatives, and your teen's friends, teachers, employer or co-workers.
- Contact local hangouts and hospitals.
- Call the police. Have an officer come to your house to take a report and pick up recent photos, dental records and fingerprints if available. Get his name, badge number and phone number; the police report number; and the name of the officer who will follow up.
- Make sure the police list your teen in the National

Crime Information Center (NCIC) to the state clearinghouse on missing children, if there is one in your state.

- Contact the National Center for Missing and Exploited Children for help with law enforcement officials — 1-800-843-5678.

- Call the Covenant House NINELINE 1-800-999-9999 for support and to check for messages. Leave a message. Also check with any local runaway hotlines.

- Contact runaway shelters locally and in nearby states.

- Make posters with photos of your teen, listing: age, height, weight, hair and eye color, complexion, physical characteristics (such as scars, birthmarks, braces or pierced ears), circumstances of disappearance, your phone number and police contacts. Distribute these to truck stops, youth-oriented businesses, hospitals, law-enforcement agencies.

- Be prepared for the first conversation with your teen. Whether in person or by phone, show concern, not anger. Say, "I love you."

- Prepare to quickly begin resolving the problems which caused your child to leave home. When your child returns home, emotions are likely to run high. Someone outside your family can help you all deal with these emotions. You may find that planned time for your teen in a temporary residence or shelter is necessary while you are resolving problems. So get outside help from a trained counselor.

Are You Out There?

Covenant House depends almost entirely on gifts from friends like you to help over 60,000 homeless and runaway children every year. We provide food, clothing, shelter, medical attention, educational and vocational training and counseling to kids with no place to go for help. Please help if you can.

YES! I want to help the kids at Covenant House. Here is my gift of: ☐ $15 ☐ $10 ☐ $25 ☐ Other

Name _____

Address _____

City _____ State _____ Zip_____

Please make your check payable to Covenant House.
Your gift is tax deductible.

☐ *Please send me your financial information.*

☐ Please send me _____ copies
of *"Sometimes God Has a Kid's Face"*

Many people like to charge their gift. If you would like to, please fill out the information below:
I prefer to charge my:
☐ **American Express** ☐ **MasterCard** ☐ **Discover** ☐ **Visa**

Account # _____

Amount _____ Exp. Date _____

Signature_____

Mail to: Covenant House
P.O. Box 96708
Washington, DC 20090-6708

Or, call 1-800-388-3888 to charge your gift on your
American Express, MasterCard, Discover or Visa.

To learn more about Covenant House and how you can help,
visit our website at www.covenanthouse.org